PICTURE LIBRARY

RIVERS AND LAKES

PICTURE LIBRARY

RIVERS AND LAKES

Norman Barrett

Franklin Watts

London   New York   Sydney   Toronto

© 1989 Franklin Watts

First published in the USA by
Franklin Watts Inc
387 Park Avenue South
New York
NY 10016

US ISBN: 0-531-10840-6
Library of Congress Catalog Card
Number 89-5713

Printed in Italy

Designed by
Barrett and Weintroub

Photographs by
N.S. Barrett
GeoScience Features
Survival Anglia
Alaska Division of Tourism
Jack Olsen/Colorado Tourism Board
Terry Farmer/Illinois DCCA
Louisiana Office of Tourism
Minnesota Office of Tourism
Peter Rabin
Malcolm A. Rose
South American Pictures
Xinghua News Agency

Illustration by
Rhoda and Robert Burns

Technical Consultant
Keith Lye

Contents

Introduction

Rivers flow across the land, from the mountains to the sea. They help to shape the land and the life of the people who live on it.

People travel on rivers and use them for transporting goods and materials. Rivers provide water for farming. Electric power is produced from some rivers, from waterfalls or by building dams. Some rivers are a source of fish, or even of precious metals like gold.

△ Pilgrims come from far and wide, by boat and on bicycle, to bathe in the Ganges River at the sacred Hindu city of Varanasi, in India.

Lakes are areas of water surrounded by land. Like rivers, they affect the lives of the people living near them. Large lakes have a cooling effect on the land in summer, and a warming influence in the colder seasons.

Rivers and lakes provide some of the world's most beautiful scenery. People enjoy many leisure activities on the water, such as swimming, boating and fishing.

△ Fishing boats on Lake Titicaca, in South America. The Aymara Indians have used these boats made of reed for hundreds of years.

7

Looking at rivers and lakes

The stages and ages of rivers
A river begins as a small stream in the mountains. Its course may be divided into three stages as it makes its way to the sea.

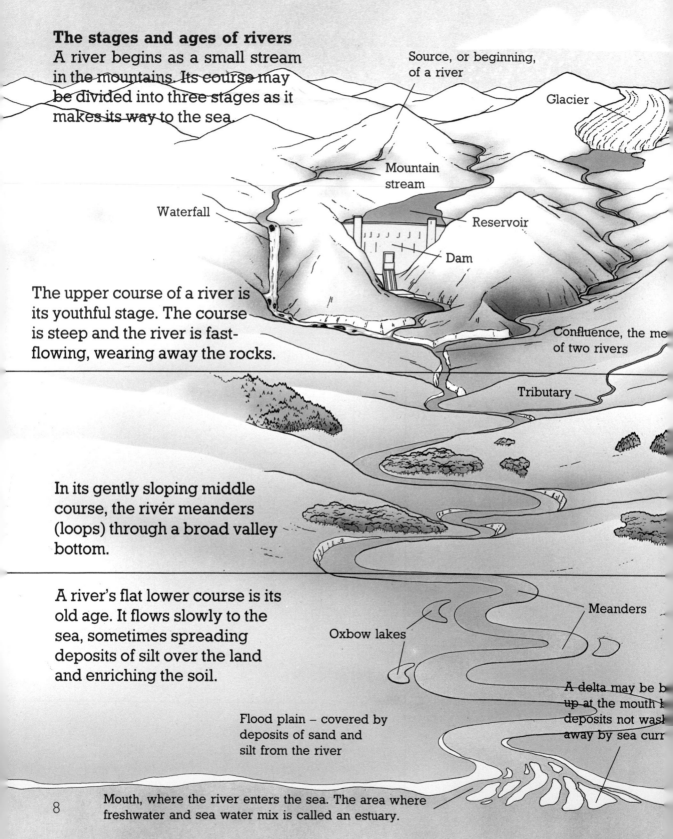

Source, or beginning, of a river

Glacier

Mountain stream

Waterfall

Reservoir

Dam

The upper course of a river is its youthful stage. The course is steep and the river is fast-flowing, wearing away the rocks.

Confluence, the me of two rivers

Tributary

In its gently sloping middle course, the river meanders (loops) through a broad valley bottom.

A river's flat lower course is its old age. It flows slowly to the sea, sometimes spreading deposits of silt over the land and enriching the soil.

Oxbow lakes

Meanders

A delta may be b up at the mouth deposits not wash away by sea curr

Flood plain – covered by deposits of sand and silt from the river

8

Mouth, where the river enters the sea. The area where freshwater and sea water mix is called an estuary.

How an oxbow lake is formed

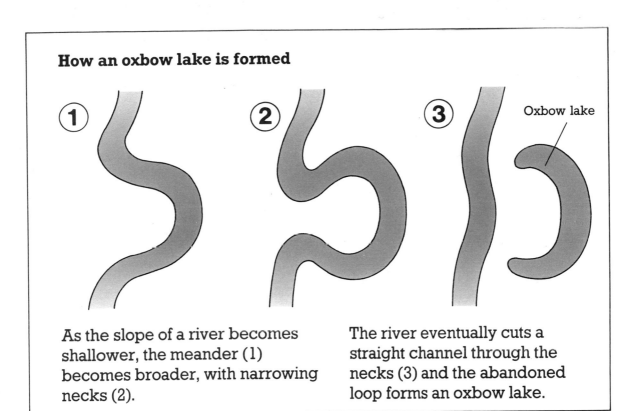

As the slope of a river becomes shallower, the meander (1) becomes broader, with narrowing necks (2).

The river eventually cuts a straight channel through the necks (3) and the abandoned loop forms an oxbow lake.

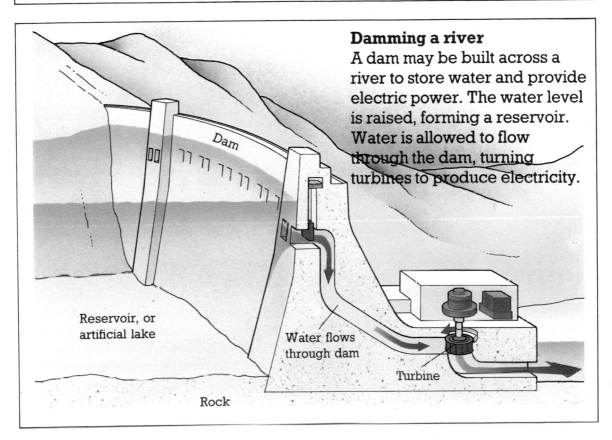

Damming a river

A dam may be built across a river to store water and provide electric power. The water level is raised, forming a reservoir. Water is allowed to flow through the dam, turning turbines to produce electricity.

Dam

Reservoir, or artificial lake

Water flows through dam

Turbine

Rock

Shaping the land

Rivers range from mighty waterways that almost cross a continent, such as the Amazon in South America, to short stretches of water. However big or small the river, it carves a valley through the land.

Not only do rivers change the shape of the land as they wear away earth and rocks. They also change the face of the land, as plant and animal life flourish, and communities of people grow up around them.

△ A fast-flowing mountain stream cuts downward, wearing out a valley in the land. Hard rocks form steps over which the river flows in a series of small waterfalls.

▷ A young river swiftly
flows along its mountain
valley. It flows around
the rocks.

▽ An aerial shot shows
an oxbow lake forming.
This is a mature stage of
a river. It develops huge
meanders, which are
eventually cut off.

△ The Colorado River cuts through the Grand Canyon, in Arizona. It is laden with silt, sand and gravel worn away from the land.

◁ A river is "braided" into several shallow channels as it winds down a flat valley floor.

The course of a river may be divided into three parts – upper, middle and lower. The upper, or youthful, course is steep and the current swift. The water carries sand and gravel, and even heavy rocks.

In its middle, or mature, course, a river's slope is gentler, but the river still wears away its banks.

In its lower, or old-age, course, the river flows slowly. It sometimes overflows its banks, and water covers the flood plain.

△ The middle course of
the Mississippi River,
with its many islands. In
its middle course, a
river carries a large
load of fine silt and mud.
Larger particles drop to
the river bed, often
building up islands.

◁ The Luangwa River,
in Zambia, southern
Africa, in flood. Heavy
rains in the upper
course of a river can
cause floods in its lower
course.

In some parts of the world, great rivers of ice move slowly along high valleys. These are glaciers. They occur in the polar regions and in mountain areas.

The ice in valley glaciers forms from compressed snow. The weight of ice forces the glacier downhill. Glaciers move only a few inches a day, but they erode deep valleys. Many rivers begin as mountain streams formed from the melting ice of glaciers.

▽ A valley glacier in Alaska winds through the mountains. Like a river, it also has tributaries.

Shaping civilization

Most of the world's big or important cities have grown up on rivers. Before rail and motor transportation, rivers were a major means of moving goods and materials across the land.

Towns grew up on river deltas and at the head of navigation, the farthest point upriver navigable by large boats. Other places suitable for the development of towns include bridging points and the confluence of two rivers.

△ London was founded at a bridging point of the Thames River. It grew up on both sides of the winding river to become at one time one of the world's busiest ports.

▷ A passenger ferry on the Nile River at Luxor, the site of Thebes, capital of ancient Egypt. Thousands of years ago, one of the world's earliest civilizations developed along the Nile valley.

▽ The Cam River flows peacefully through Cambridge, in England. The town flourished as a river port, at the head of navigation, before becoming famous for its university.

How lakes are formed

Most of the world's lakes lie in areas that were once covered by glaciers. These wore out deep valleys and hollows. When the glaciers melted, their waters were often dammed behind rocks dumped by the glaciers, forming lakes.

Thousands of these glacial lakes can be found in Scandinavia, Canada and the northern parts of the United States. The Great Lakes, in North America, were formed partly by melting glaciers.

△ A lake in Norway, formed originally by melting glaciers.

Some lakes form when rivers straighten their course. The old bend is left as an oxbow lake. Eventually the water dries up and becomes a swamp.

Other lakes form in deep valleys created by earth movements. Some form when landslides or lava from volcanoes form natural dams, blocking river valleys.

Lakes are also formed when rain or spring water fills the craters of extinct volcanoes.

▽ Crater Lake, in Oregon, lies in the caldera formed by the explosion and collapse of the volcano Mount Mazama, which erupted nearly 7,000 years ago. The lake was formed by rain and snow. Its greatest depth is 589 m (1,932 ft).

◁ Lake Natron, in Tanzania, lies in the Great Rift Valley in eastern Africa. Its waters, which have been described as "soda slush," come from springs arising from inside a volcano.

▽ A "lake" drying out in Saudi Arabia. This country is a desert, with no permanent rivers or lakes. But rare rainstorms fill the flat-bottomed valleys called wadis with water, which eventually evaporates or soaks into the ground.

Controlling nature

Rivers are among the great forces of nature. In many parts of the world, they have been controlled to make use of the water or to prevent it from causing a disaster.

Many rivers have been dammed to harness the energy of the water for producing electricity, or to store the water for irrigation.

The building of a dam creates an artificial lake, which serves as a water store, or reservoir.

△ The Bagnell Dam, on the Osage River in Missouri, created the Lake of the Ozarks. A river is raised to a higher level by a dam, and the water forms a lake. Water is allowed through the dam so that the river may continue its course. At the same time, it turns turbines in the dam to produce electricity.

When a dam is built, the surrounding land is deliberately flooded. Rivers in their lower course often flood the land, spreading silt over the flood plain and enriching the soil. But in some places steps have to be taken to keep a river from overflowing.

Floods are caused when heavy rainfall or the sudden melting of snow and ice raises the level of a river above its banks. A river's banks may be built up to prevent floods that endanger life and land.

▽ Lake Powell, one of the largest artificial lakes in the world, is a popular recreation area. It was created by the damming of the Colorado River in northern Arizona, but lies mainly in the state of Utah.

△ The Mississippi River, near New Orleans, is flanked by levees. These are wide walls built along the banks to keep the river from flooding.

▷ The Thames Barrier, built across the river at Woolwich, southeast London. It may be closed to prevent the flooding of London in the event of a sudden surge back of water upriver from its mouth.

At work and play

Rivers and lakes around the world are used by people for leisure activities. All kinds of sports take place on the water. The surrounding areas, especially of lakes, make ideal resorts.

Factories and mines are often based by rivers and lakes, which provide convenient and cheap transportation. But chemicals and other waste dumped in rivers can cause serious health hazards.

▷ A small local industry – washing clothes on the banks of the Lima River, in Portugal.

▽ Waste from mining works has polluted this river in Peru. Pollution of rivers and lakes by the dumping of industrial waste has become a serious problem throughout the world.

△ Barges carry material and goods along the Mississippi River, at Baton Rouge, Louisiana.

◁ Rafting on the rapids of the Arkansas River, in Colorado.

Living by rivers and lakes

△ Flamingos flock to Lake Nakuru, in eastern Africa, to breed. Wildlife is abundant on, in and around rivers and lakes. It includes mammals such as beavers and otters, as well as fish and water birds.

◁ A poor Brazilian family in their shack, built on stilts on the side of the great Amazon River. People also live on riverboats in towns and in luxury lakeside homes.

The story of rivers and lakes

Life on the Nile

One of the world's first great civilizations grew up along the Nile River more than 5,000 years ago, when two kingdoms united in 3100 BC as the nation of Egypt. It flourished as a great power for over 2,000 years.

Egypt owed its greatness to the floodwaters of the Nile. Every year the river deposited rich, black soil on the land. Farmers were able to grow two or three crops a year on the fertile soil.

The Dead Sea

Another body of water known from ancient times is the Dead Sea. This is a saltwater lake, which forms parts of the border between Israel and Jordan. It was first mentioned in the Bible in the Book of Genesis as the "Salt Sea." It is nearly ten times as salty as the oceans.

△ Victoria Falls, on the border of Zimbabwe and Zambia, is one of the world's natural wonders.

Natural wonders

People are fond of listing the "seven wonders of the world," ancient, modern or natural. Rivers and lakes often rate high on lists of natural wonders.

Among the most spectacular are the great waterfalls, especially Victoria Falls in southern Africa. The Grand Canyon of the Colorado River is always high on any list, and Crater Lake, in Oregon, is also regarded as a natural wonder.

△ The Dead Sea, a saltwater lake, is the saltiest body of water in the world

China's Sorrow

The Yellow River, or Hwang He, is sometimes known as "China's Sorrow" because of the death and destruction its floods have caused over the years. In 1887, nearly a million people lost their lives when its muddy waters overflowed and covered an area of 130,000 sq km (50,000 sq mi).

△ A pumping station on the Yellow River. Muddy water from the river has the sand filtered out, and the clear water is then pumped up to irrigate crops on high land.

It is called the Yellow River because of the large amounts of yellow earth it carries. Millions of people depend on its waters to irrigate the land. Dikes have been built along the river to prevent flooding, but it has never been completely controlled.

Old Man River

The Mississippi River runs down the center of the United States, from northern Minnesota to the Gulf of Mexico. On its way, it is joined by more than 250 tributaries.

The Mississippi has played an important part in the history of the United States. It is known affectionately as "Old Man River" to the millions of people who live on or near its banks, in big cities that have grown up along it and on the plantations and farms it irrigates.

Early settlers came by raft and boat to make their homes in the valley. Later on, paddle-wheeled steamboats were used for trade, and the river is still one of the greatest trading waterways in the world. But as well as bringing prosperity, it has also brought disaster. Flooding has caused many deaths and much damage to property and land.

△ A paddle-wheeled steamer on the Mississippi gives tourists a taste of the river's rich past.

Facts and records

The longest river

The courses of rivers change and it is often difficult to establish where their main channels run and exactly where their sources are. So people argue about which is the world's longest river: the Amazon in South America or the Nile in Africa. Both are about 6,500 km (4,000 miles) long.

△ Niagara Falls, illuminated at night, is a great tourist attraction.

△ A floating village on the Amazon, one of the world's longest rivers.

Waterfalls

Waterfalls provide some of the most spectacular sights in nature, as a river plunges dramatically from one level to another.

The world's highest falls are the Angel Falls, in Venezuela, where the Carrao River drops a total of 979 m (3,212 ft).

At times, the Boyoma Falls in Zaire carry millions of tons of water per minute between levels of the Zaire River. Other waterfalls where huge volumes of water cascade over high cliffs include the Iguaçu Falls, on the Brazil-Argentina border, and Niagara Falls, between Canada and the United States.

Highest Lake

There are small lakes near the peaks of some of the world's highest mountains, but the highest large lake is Titicaca, in South America. Surrounded by the Andes Mountains, Lake Titicaca lies in both Peru and Bolivia. It is 3,812 m (12,507 ft) above sea level.

△ The town of Copacabana, in Bolivia, lies on the shore of Lake Titicaca, the world's highest lake.

Glossary

Caldera
A very large volcano crater.

Confluence
The point where two rivers come together.

Dam
A natural or artificial barrier that blocks or controls a river's flow.

Delta
A flat-topped structure of sediments deposited where the speed of a river slows as it enters a quieter body of water.

Dike
A wall or bank built to prevent a river from overflowing.

Flood plain
The part of a river valley containing the river channel, and also the surrounding flat area of sediments deposited when the river overflows its banks.

Glacier
A mass of ice moving slowly down a valley.

Irrigation
The artificial distribution of water over land for the purpose of growing crops.

Levee
The natural bank of a river formed by sand and other deposits during flooding. Artificial levees are also built to keep a river in its channel.

Meander
A curve or loop in the course of a river.

Mouth
The place where a river enters a sea or a lake.

Oxbow lake
A lake formed when a meander of a river is cut off.

Rapids
A stretch of river where the current flows faster than its normal speed, caused by a sudden steepening of its course.

Silt
A deposit, finer than sand and coarser than clay, laid down in a river.

Source
The place where a river begins.

Tributary
A river or stream that flows into a larger river.

Index